Ages and Timelines

Subtraction on the Open Number Line

Catherine Twomey Fosnot

*first*hand
An imprint of Heinemann
A division of Reed Elsevier, Inc.
361 Hanover Street
Portsmouth, NH 03801–3912
firsthand.heinemann.com

Offices and agents throughout the world

ISBN 13: 978-0-325-01014-4
ISBN 10: 0-325-01014-5

Harcourt School Publishers
6277 Sea Harbor Drive
Orlando, FL 32887–6777
www.harcourtschool.com

ISBN 13: 978-0-15-360566-6
ISBN 10: 0-15-360566-9

© 2007 Catherine Twomey Fosnot

The development of a portion of the material described within was supported in part
by the National Science Foundation under Grant No. 9911841. Any opinions, findings,
and conclusions or recommendations expressed in these materials are those of the
authors and do not necessarily reflect the views of the National Science Foundation.

Library of Congress Cataloging-in-Publication Data
CIP data is on file with the Library of Congress

Printed in the United States of America on acid-free paper

11 10 09 08 07   ML   1 2 3 4 5 6

Acknowledgements

Photography

Herbert Seignoret
Mathematics in the City, City College of New York

Illustrator

Margaret Sanfilippo Lindmark

Schools featured in photographs

The Muscota New School/PS 314 (an empowerment school in Region 10), New York, NY
Independence School/PS 234 (Region 9), New York, NY
Fort River Elementary School, Amherst, MA

Contents

Unit Overview

This unit begins with the story of Carlos, an eight-year-old boy who is fascinated by his great-grandfather's thick, beautiful silver hair. His great-grandfather lives in Puerto Rico and Carlos is preparing to meet him for the first time. Having only seen photos of him as a much younger man, Carlos wonders how old his great-grandfather is and how many years it will take before he might have hair like that, too. As Carlos begins to investigate these questions, his whole family becomes involved in exploring age differences and figuring out how old they each were when Carlos was born. When Carlos shares his investigation with his teacher, the whole school gets involved in the project.

This story context sets the stage for a series of investigations in this unit. Children interview their family members and compare age differences. Timelines are introduced as a context for using the open number line—a helpful model used as a tool to explore and represent strategies for addition and subtraction. This unit will focus on the open number line as a model for subtraction.

The Landscape of Learning

BIG IDEAS

- The relationship between addition and subtraction
- Generalization of subtraction as removal, as difference, and as used to find missing addends and subtrahends
- Constant difference as equivalence
- The place value patterns that occur when adding and subtracting groups of ten

STRATEGIES

- Counting on and counting backward
- Taking leaps of ten
- Decomposing to get a landmark number
- Splitting
- Adding on vs. removing
- Using constant difference

MODEL

- Open number line

In contrast to a number line with counting numbers written below, an "open" number line is just an empty line used to record children's addition and subtraction strategies. Only the numbers that children use are recorded and the addition and subtraction are recorded as leaps or jumps. For example, if a child's strategy for adding 8 + 79 is 79 + 1 + 7, using a landmark number of 80, it would be recorded on the open number line as:

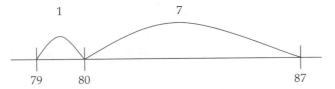

The recording would be similar if a child solves 87 − 8 by first removing 7 and then 1. Modeling children's thinking on the open number line helps them move beyond counting on by ones for addition and subtraction, to strategies such as taking leaps of ten, decomposing, and/or using landmark numbers. Use of the open number line also encourages discussion of the relationship between addition and subtraction and of the relationship between various problems in which the operation of subtraction can be employed—such as removal, comparative difference, and finding a missing addend.

As the unit progresses, timelines are used to record years of birth, rather than ages. This change in context challenges learners to grapple with larger numbers and with the changing places of the part-whole relations of numbers on the number line. For example, first the number 79 may be marked on the number line as 8 less than 87; then it may be the difference between 2005 and 1926.

Several minilessons for subtraction are also included in the unit. These are structured using strings of related problems as a way to guide learners more explicitly toward computational fluency with subtraction.

Note: It is expected that children will have had substantial experience with number lines prior to this unit. If this is not the case, you might want to take a look at the unit *Measuring for the Art Show*, to see how the number line model can be developed.

The Mathematical Landscape

Research has documented that the open number line better aligns with children's invented strategies than base-ten blocks and the hundred chart, and it stimulates a mental representation of numbers and number operations that is more powerful for developing mental arithmetic strategies. Children using the open number line are cognitively involved in their actions. In contrast, children who use base-ten blocks or the hundred chart sometimes tend to depend primarily on visualization, which results in a passive "reading off" behavior, rather than cognitive involvement in the actions undertaken (Klein, Beishuizen, and Treffers 2002).

Research has also documented that children initially use a variety of very different actions when they subtract because they perceive subtraction story problems in very different ways depending on the context (Carpenter, Fennema, Peterson, Chiang, and Loef 1989). Therefore, helping them generalize the operation across different contexts—exploring how the problems are related—is an important goal.

This unit, which is based on the research referenced above, is designed to support the development of several big ideas and strategies related to subtraction. The open number line model is employed throughout as a tool for thinking.

BIG IDEAS

This unit is designed to encourage the development of some of the big ideas underlying a deep understanding of subtraction:

❖ *the relationship between addition and subtraction*

❖ *generalization of subtraction as removal, as difference, and as used to find missing addends and subtrahends*

❖ *constant difference as equivalence*

❖ *the place value patterns that occur when adding and subtracting groups of ten*

❖ The relationship between addition and subtraction

Subtraction is the inverse of addition. But young children often initially approach addition and subtraction contexts with nothing more than counting strategies in their repertoire. They have not yet realized that addition and subtraction are related—that part-whole relations are involved. If $79 + 8 = 87$, then it necessarily follows that $87 - 8 = 79$. Young children may notice that the numbers are "switched" but it may seem like magic or a trick way to check answers. Several investigations and minilessons in this unit were designed to make the relationship between addition and subtraction explicit.

❖ Generalization of subtraction as removal, as difference, and as used to find missing addends and subtrahends

When children have not constructed an understanding of part-whole relations, subtraction problems in different contexts are subsequently seen as unrelated. For example, consider these problems:

(1) My mom is 33 and I am 8; how many more years will it be until I am 33?

(2) How old was my mom when I was born?

(3) What's the difference in our ages?

(4) How many years ago was my mom 8?

The table below shows how children typically mathematize these situations.

QUESTION	DESCRIPTION	COMMENT
How many more years will it be until I am 33?	missing addend	suggests adding on
How old was my mom when I was born?	removal	suggests removing or counting back 8
What's the difference in our ages?	difference	suggests two separate groups to be compared
How many years ago was my mom 8?	missing subtrahend	suggests counting backward to 8, while keeping track of the result

How is it that children ever come to realize that these problems are related, particularly when their actions to solve them are so different? Generalization of subtraction as removal, as difference, and as an operation to find missing addends and subtrahends is critical for a deep understanding of subtraction. Thus, it is important to engage children in exploring all varieties of subtraction contexts where the numbers are the same. The resulting patterns will cause children to wonder how the problems are related and give you opportunities to push for generalization.

❖ Constant difference as equivalence

Constant difference—whatever you add to one number you must add to the other to maintain an equivalent difference between the numbers—is an important big idea for subtraction that children need to construct. As children developed strategies for addition in other units of this series (see *Bunk Beds and Apple Boxes*), they most likely constructed the idea of compensation—that if you lose 1 (from 5, for example) but gain it (onto 3), the total stays the same: $5 + 3 = 4 + 4$. They may try this for subtraction and be surprised when it doesn't work: $71 - 36$ is not equivalent to $70 - 37$. With subtraction, the difference must be kept constant. If my mom is 33 and I am 8, the difference between our ages will still be the same when she is 35 and I am 10: $33 - 8 = 35 - 10$. It is important that you allow children to explore these ideas and to puzzle over when, and why, they work. Doing so will only deepen their understanding of the part-whole relations involved. When constant difference is deeply understood it can become a terrific mental math strategy: $71 - 36$ might be difficult for children, but $70 - 35$ is much easier!

❖ The place value patterns that occur when adding and subtracting groups of ten

Once children have an understanding of the landmark decade numbers in our number system, they can easily count forward and backward by 10: 80, 70, 60, etc. But subtracting 10 from 82 is often another story. They are frequently surprised by the place value pattern that results when one repeatedly subtracts 10: 72, 62, 52, 42, etc. Knowledge of this pattern and why it occurs is an important big idea connected to place value that is also critical to the development of efficient subtraction strategies. For example, in solving 82 − 19, we often wish children would just mentally think: 72, 62, plus 1, 63. But without a deep knowledge of place value and the patterns that result when subtracting groups of ten, this is not an easy strategy. Although the focus of this unit is not on the development of place value per se, several minilessons are used in the first week to explore and remind children of the patterns that result when subtracting groups of ten. (The units in this series that focus more specifically on developing place value are *Organizing and Collecting,* and *The T-Shirt Factory.*)

STRATEGIES

As you work with the activities in this unit, you will also notice that children will use many strategies to subtract. Some strategies to notice are:

❖ *counting on and counting backward*

❖ *taking leaps of ten*

❖ *decomposing to get to a landmark number*

❖ *splitting*

❖ *adding on vs. removing*

❖ *using constant difference*

❖ Counting on and counting backward

Subtracting effectively and efficiently requires that children have a repertoire of many strategies and a good enough sense of number and operation that they look to the numbers first before they decide on an appropriate strategy. Initially children rely on counting, both counting on and counting backward: to solve 33 − 8, they might count backward—32, 31, 30, 29, 28, 27, 26, 25—or they might count on from 8. While these strategies may be very appropriate in the beginning stages of the development of subtraction, they are only starting places. Such strategies are tedious and open up many opportunities for losing track and other errors. Teachers often think a pencil and paper strategy with regrouping is the next step. This is not true. There are many steps in between.

❖ Taking leaps of ten

As the big ideas for subtraction are being constructed, you will want to encourage children to make use of them for computation. One of the first strategies to encourage is taking leaps of ten—solving 72−33 as 62, 52, 42, 41, 40, 39. Although this is still tedious, it is a bit more efficient than counting by ones and, by using it, children will eventually develop the ability to remove the 30 all at once (followed by the 3) and, when removing numbers close to landmarks, such as 29, to remove 30 and then add 1 back in.

❖ Decomposing to get to a landmark number

Children will often also decompose a subtrahend to get themselves to a landmark number—they may solve 72 − 33 by first decomposing the 33 into 30 + 2 + 1, then removing 2 to get to 70, then removing 30 to get to 40, and finally removing the last 1, for a result of 39. It is important for you to notice these emerging strategies and celebrate children's developing number sense!

❖ Splitting

Another way children often decompose is by using expanded notation—they split the numbers using the columns. To solve 72 − 33, they think of 72 as 70 + 2, and 33 as 30 + 3. They find the differences first within the columns and then combine the partial differences: 70 − 30 = 40; 2 − 3 = −1; 40 − 1 = 39. When children are taught the traditional algorithm prematurely they often say, "Two minus three is one." This behavior rarely occurs when children are asked to make sense of the situation for themselves, and splitting strategies go a long way in helping children understand negative numbers later on.

❖ Adding on vs. removing

Note when children begin to vary adding on and removing—for example, when the numbers are close together (32 − 28) it is helpful to think of adding on from 28, but when they are far apart (32 − 4), it is more efficient to just go back 4. Knowing that this is OK to do, however, is based on the big ideas of generalizing the operation across various problems and understanding the relationship of addition to subtraction. A long-term objective on the horizon of the landscape of learning for subtraction is for children to look to the numbers first before deciding on a strategy. Mathematicians do not use the same strategy for every problem; their strategies vary depending on the numbers.

❖ Using constant difference

Perhaps the most difficult strategy for children to use is constant difference—sliding the numbers up or down the number line while keeping the difference constant, to make the problem friendly. Yet this is one of the most powerful mental math strategies that mathematicians use. For example, 132 − 89 is easily solved by adding 11 to both numbers: 143 − 100.

This unit was carefully crafted and field-tested to ensure that constant difference is specifically addressed. Not only will a discussion of constant difference come up as children explore age differences, but minilessons are included to support the use of this idea as a strategy.

MATHEMATICAL MODELING

The model developed in this unit is the open number line. This model supports children in envisioning the relationship of addition and subtraction, and they are able to explore how the various subtraction contexts are related. The model also supports the development of the various strategies for computational fluency.

Models go through three stages of development (Gravemeijer 1999; Fosnot and Dolk 2001):

- ❖ *model of the situation*

- ❖ *model of children's strategies*

- ❖ *model as a tool for thinking*

❖ Model of the situation

Initially models grow out of modeling a situation. In this unit, the open number line emerges as a timeline used for exploring age differences.

❖ Model of children's strategies

Children benefit from seeing the teacher model their strategies. Once a model has been introduced to represent the situation, you can use it to model

children's strategies as they explain their thinking. If a child solves 33 − 8 by removing 10 and then adding 2 back in, draw the following:

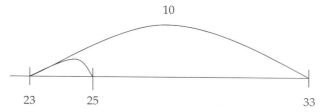

If a child says, "I made the problem friendly. I turned it into 35 − 10," draw the following:

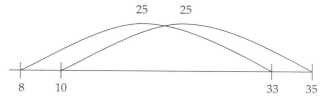

Representations like these give children a chance to discuss and envision each other's strategies.

❖ Model as a tool for thinking

Eventually children become able to use the open number line as a tool for thinking—to prove and explore their ideas, such as why constant difference works.

Many opportunities to discuss these landmarks in mathematical development will arise as you work through this unit. Look for moments of puzzlement. Don't hesitate to let children discuss their ideas, and check and recheck their strategies. Celebrate their accomplishments just as you would a toddler's first steps when learning to walk!

A graphic of the full landscape of learning for early number sense, addition, and subtraction is provided on page 11. The purpose of this graphic is to allow you to see the longer journey of children's mathematical development and to place your work with this unit within the scope of this long-term development. You may also find it helpful to use this graphic as a way to record the progress of individual children for yourself. Each landmark can be shaded in as you find evidence in a child's work and in what the child says—evidence that a landmark strategy, big idea, or way of modeling has been constructed. In a sense you will be recording the individual pathways children take as they develop as young mathematicians!

References and Resources

Carpenter, Thomas P., Elizabeth Fennema, Penelope L. Peterson, Chi-Pang Chiang, and Megan Loef. 1989. Using knowledge of children's mathematics thinking in classroom teaching: An experimental study. *American Education Research Journal, 26*, 499–553.

Dolk, Maarten and Catherine Twomey Fosnot. 2004a. *Addition and Subtraction Minilessons, Grades PreK–3.* CD-ROM with accompanying facilitator's guide by Antonia Cameron, Sherrin B. Hersch, and Catherine Twomey Fosnot. Portsmouth, NH: Heinemann.

———. 2004b. *Exploring Ages, Grades PreK–3: The Role of Context.* CD-ROM with accompanying facilitator's guide by Antonia Cameron, Sherrin B. Hersch, and Catherine Twomey Fosnot. Portsmouth, NH: Heinemann.

———. 2004c. *Fostering Children's Mathematical Development, Grades PreK–3: The Landscape of Learning.* CD-ROM with accompanying facilitator's guide by Sherrin B. Hersch, Antonia Cameron, and Catherine Twomey Fosnot. Portsmouth, NH: Heinemann.

Fosnot, Catherine Twomey and Maarten Dolk. 2001. *Young Mathematicians at Work: Constructing Number Sense, Addition, and Subtraction.* Portsmouth, NH: Heinemann.

Gravemeijer, Koeno P.E. 1999. How emergent models may foster the constitution of formal mathematics. *Mathematical Thinking and Learning 1(2),* 155–77.

Karlin, Samuel. 1983. Eleventh R. A. Fisher Memorial Lecture. *Royal Society 20.*

Klein, Anton S., Meindert Beishuizen, and Adri Treffers. 2002. The empty number line in Dutch second grade. In *Lessons Learned from Research,* eds. Judith Sowder and Bonnie Schapelle. Reston, VA: National Council of Teachers of Mathematics.

NUMBER SENSE, ADDITION, and SUBTRACTION

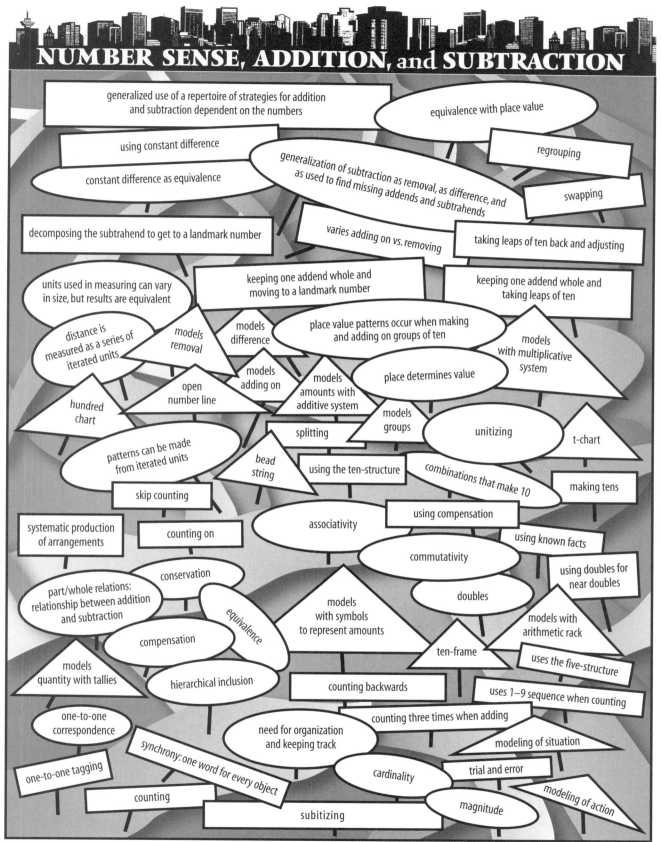

The landscape of learning: number sense, addition, and subtraction on the horizon showing landmark strategies (rectangles), big ideas (ovals), and models (triangles).

DAY ONE

Exploring Ages

The context of age differences is developed with the story *El Bisabuelo Gregorio.* The open number line is introduced as a tool to explore the age differences of the characters in the story and then children work in pairs to compile data. A subsequent math congress provides a forum for discussing children's strategies and interesting patterns that appear in the data.

Day One Outline

Developing the Context

* Read *El Bisabuelo Gregorio* up to the point when Carlos figures out Bisabuelo Gregorio's age.
* Ask the children for other ways to figure out Bisabuelo Gregorio's age and record their strategies on an open number line.
* Finish the story and then with the children reconstruct the data from page 9 and post it on a chart.

Supporting the Investigation

* Support and challenge children as they investigate the questions in Appendix B.

Preparing for the Math Congress

* Observe the various subtraction strategies children use.
* Plan to scaffold a congress discussion that will move from less efficient strategies to more efficient strategies.

Facilitating the Math Congress

* Record the children's strategies on an open number line.
* Discuss the patterns that arise in the data as you fill in the chart created earlier.

Materials Needed

El Bisabuelo Gregorio [If you do not have the full-color read-aloud book (available from Heinemann), you can use Appendix A.]

Student recording sheets for the exploring ages investigation (Appendix B)—one set per pair of children

Drawing paper—several sheets per pair of children

Large chart pad and easel (or chalkboard or whiteboard)

Markers

Developing the Context

☀ Read *El Bisabuelo Gregorio* up to the point when Carlos figures out Bisabuelo Gregorio's age.

☀ Ask the children for other ways to figure out Bisabuelo Gregorio's age and record their strategies on an open number line.

☀ Finish the story and then with the children reconstruct the data from page 9 and post it on a chart.

Read *El Bisabuelo Gregorio* (Appendix A) until the story describes how Carlos figures out Bisabuelo Gregorio's age. After you say, "Was he right?" ask the children what they think. Before you continue with the story, draw a timeline (an open number line) on chart paper. After you explain to the children what it is, tell them that you will make a picture of Carlos's strategy on it. Use the timeline like an open number line and place 79 on it. Represent Carlos's strategy by making a jump of 1 to get to 80, then a jump of 7 more. Mark 87 where you land.

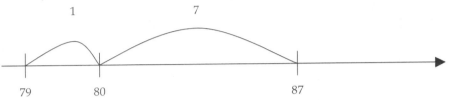

Ask the children if any of them figured this out a different way and model their strategies on the timeline, too. For example, some of the children may have started with 8, added 9, and then 70 more:

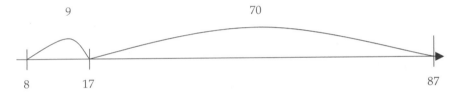

Others may have started at 8, added 80 and then removed 1:

Encourage the children to discuss the recordings and the strategies and ensure that they agree with Carlos's answer before you continue reading.

The purpose for introducing the timeline here is to suggest it as a tool for thinking when children go off to investigate later. When you have finished reading, suggest that the children work on investigating the ages of Carlos's other family members. It is likely that they will be excited and will want to start investigating their own families. They will have the opportunity to do so later in this unit; however, it is important to begin with everyone working with the same data. For this reason, the first part of this unit focuses solely on the characters in the story.

With the children, reconstruct the data on Carlos's family from page 9 and post it on chart paper:

	Carlos	Maria	Mamá	Papá	Grandpa Juan	Grandma Rosita	Bisabuelo Gregorio
Current age	8	10	33	35	55	57	87

Ask the children to investigate the following questions:

- How old was everyone when Carlos was born?
- How old was everyone when Maria was born?

Supporting the Investigation

Assign math partners and give each pair of children one set of recording sheets (Appendix B). Also provide blank paper for working and suggest that they might find it helpful to draw timelines. Space is provided on the recording sheets for this purpose as well. As children work, walk around and confer with them as needed to support and challenge their investigation. Have children put their recording sheets in their work folders when they are done.

☀ Support and challenge children as they investigate the questions in Appendix B.

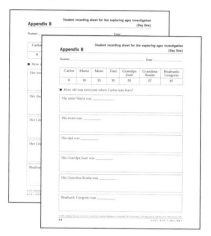

Conferring with Students at Work

Inside One Classroom

Juan: I think we have to add.

Manuel: No. Subtract.

Juan: Subtract? What do we subtract?

Manuel: Let's do the mom first. I think we have to do 33 minus 8.

Juan: Oh yeah. 'Cause we want to know 8 years ago. How old she was then. That is when Carlos was born. So 32, 31, 30…
(Keeping track on his fingers.)

Matt (the teacher): Let's draw a number line and try to do it in jumps. How many from 33 to 30?

Juan: Three.

Matt: So I'll mark those. How many more to go? We need to go back 8 and you said we've only done 3 so far, right?

Continued on next page

Author's Notes

Many children often count back when subtracting, more from habit than necessity. By suggesting jumps and supporting them by keeping track on the number line, Matt is encouraging them to become more efficient. He is also offering a helpful model as a tool to think with.

Continued from previous page

Juan: Yup, 5 more.

Matt: *(To Manuel.)* Do you agree?

Manuel: *(Nods.)* 25!

Matt: Okay. So work on the other people now and I'll check back with you later.

During the investigation, Matt will most likely only sit with four or five pairs to confer. He also moves around the room, taking note of the kinds of strategies that are being used. Children can work autonomously and they are learning even when the teacher is not there because they are discussing and reflecting with their partners.

Preparing for the Math Congress

☀ Observe the various subtraction strategies children used.

☀ Plan to scaffold a congress discussion that will move from less efficient strategies to more efficient strategies.

As you move around the room, take note of the various subtraction strategies being used. Here are some strategies you might see:

✦ Counting backward by ones and keeping track with fingers, e.g., for 55 − 8: 54, 53, 52, 51,…47.

✦ Decomposing the 8 to get to a landmark number, e.g., 55 − 8 = 55 − 5 − 3. In this case, 50 is the landmark number.

✦ Subtracting 10 and adding 2 back in, e.g., 55 − 10 + 2.

✦ Noting and making use of patterns and equivalent relations: People were always 2 years older when Carlos was born than when Maria was born (since Maria is 10).

■ Tips for Structuring the Math Congress

It might be helpful to scaffold this congress by moving from less efficient strategies, such as counting backward by ones, to more efficient strategies, such as using landmark numbers or using tens. By noting which strategies children have used, you can make a decision about which children you will have share and the order in which they will share. As you prepare, try to imagine how the conversation will flow.

Facilitating the Math Congress

Convene the children in the meeting area to discuss their strategies. Have them sit next to their partners with their recording sheets. Explain that as they share their strategies, you will represent them on a timeline. Start the sharing with someone who counted backward by ones. A counting backward strategy on the number line is represented as follows:

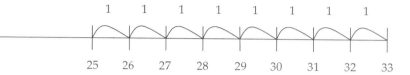

Have just one or two children share this strategy, i.e., how old the mom and dad were when Carlos was born.

Next, ask a group that has decomposed the 8 and used landmark numbers to share. Use the initial number line. With a different color marker show the jumps and have a discussion on this strategy, highlighting its efficiency.

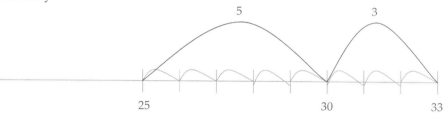

As this strategy is shared, encourage the children who counted by ones to explain the jumps. Have them try a few of the other problems using a jumping strategy.

Use the chart you made earlier, filling it in as the congress progresses:

	Carlos	Maria	Mamá	Papá	Grandpa Juan	Grandma Rosita	Bisabuelo Gregorio
Current age	8	10	33	35	55	57	87
Age at Carlos's birth		2	25	27	47	49	79
Age at Maria's birth			23	25	45	47	77

Once the chart is complete, suggest that the children look at it and discuss any patterns that they notice. Specifically, encourage children to look at the difference of 2 when comparing the data for Carlos and Maria, e.g., 25 and 23, 27 and 25, 47 and 45, etc.

	Carlos	Maria	Mamá	Papá	Grandpa Juan	Grandma Rosita	Bisabuelo Gregorio
Current age	8	10	33	35	55	57	87
Age at Carlos's birth		2	25	27	47	49	79
Age at Maria's birth			23	25	45	47	77

☀ Record the children's strategies on an open number line.

☀ Discuss the patterns that arise in the data as you fill in the chart created earlier.

If children do not notice this pattern, you can offer it yourself. Encourage them to think about why this difference of two is happening. Ask them if there might be a way to use the data for Maria (the third row) to produce the data for Carlos (the second row). If any of the children have used a strategy of taking 10 away (from the ages in the first row) and then adding 2 back in as a way to subtract 8 (to determine the ages in the second row), you can have them discuss their strategy now and then explore the context of the two-year age difference as a way to help other children understand why this strategy works.

A Portion of the Math Congress

Matt (the teacher): Ian, would you and Peter begin? Tell us how you figured out how old Carlos's mom was when he was born.

Ian: She was 25. We counted: 32, 31, 30, 29, 28, 27, 26, 25.

Matt: I'll make a picture of your strategy on the timeline. *(He draws timeline.)* And you did the same strategy for figuring out how old the dad was?

Peter: Yup. He was 27. We counted: 34, 33, 32, 31, 30, 29, 28, 27.

Matt: Does everyone agree with Peter and Ian? Questions or comments for them? You did a lot of work. I wonder if there are any shortcuts? Amirah?

Amirah: We counted to figure out the mom, too. But we noticed that the dad was 2 years older, so we didn't have to subtract for the dad. We just added 2.

Matt: That is interesting. Turn to the person next to you. Why can Amirah just add 2? Does that work? *(Allows some pair talk time.)* Ian, Peter, what do you think about that?

Ian: It works! He is 2 years older than the mom, so you just add 2!

Matt: So I can just add 2 more on the number line? If I start at 35, instead of 33? Wow! Isn't that a nice shortcut! As mathematicians we love these efficient, clever ways, don't we? I noticed that Marcus and Sally had a neat shortcut, too. Would you both go next? Tell us what you did and I'll make a picture on the timeline.

Sally: We made jumps. For the mom we made a jump of 3 and then 5.

Author's Notes

By starting with children who counted laboriously by ones, Matt invites the children in the congress to consider helpful ways to proceed besides counting.

Drawing the strategy on the number line provides a visual representation of the strategy. Over time the model will become a tool to think with.

By asking the children for pair talk, Matt engages all of them in considering the pattern, and he pushes the children to explain what is happening.

Continued on next page

Continued from previous page

Matt: *(Draws on the original number line.)* So you didn't even count at all! You used friendly numbers to help you. Let's all try your strategy for Grandpa Juan. He is 55. What is a nice friendly number to get to?

Several voices: Fifty!

Matt: Ok, let me draw that, a jump of 5! How many more to go? Ian?

Ian: Three.

Matt: Does everyone agree that we have 3 more to go? So how old was he?

Marcus: He was 47.

Matt: So let's get our chart filled in. We've got some nice strategies and we can check our answers as we fill in the chart. *(He continues, requesting answers, filling in the chart as children check. When disagreement occurs, strategies are checked.)* Let's all look at the chart now. Turn to the person next to you. Share what you noticed.

Yolanda: The dad is always 2 more, like we said. And the grandma is always 2 more than the grandpa, 'cause she is 2 years older than him.

Gabrielle: We noticed that Maria's results go in twos too—2 less than Carlos. The mom is 23, not 25. The dad is 25, not 27.

Yolanda: 'Cause Maria is 2 years older than Carlos!

Matt: That's interesting. Could we use Maria's results and then add 2 each time to get Carlos's results? Talk to your neighbor about this. Could Carlos always use Maria's age of 10 to help?

Drawing the strategy on the original number line provides children with a visual representation of the connection between the strategies.

Pair talk provides for focused reflection. Implicitly Matt's action says, "Mathematicians notice and discuss interesting numerical patterns."

▨ Assessment Tips

Take a look at the children's recording sheets and their scrap paper. Note their strategies, such as whether they are counting back by ones, decomposing, or taking leaps of ten and noticing the connections between Carlos's data and Maria's. It is helpful to jot down your observations on sticky notes. Later, you can place these on children's recording sheets to be included in their portfolios.

Differentiating Instruction

By allowing children to mathematize this situation in their own ways, you can be assured that you are differentiating appropriately. As the congress discussion progresses, also be alert for moments when you can stretch and challenge as well as moments when you need to pull children into the discussion to ensure that they understand. Use the context to help children realize the meaning of what they are doing—i.e., talk about a year ago, two years ago, etc.—and use the timeline.

Reflections on the Day

Today children were introduced to the context of age differences. As children worked with the data in the story *El Bisabuelo Gregorio,* they utilized and discussed a variety of strategies for subtraction. The open number line was used to represent the strategies and children discussed patterns in the data. This discussion encouraged children to consider how 10 might be used, for example how subtracting 8 is equivalent to subtracting 10 and adding 2. It also set the stage for exploring two different uses of subtraction: removal and difference.

Exploring Ages

A minilesson on taking leaps of ten for both addition and subtraction engages children in thinking about place value patterns and using them when figuring out differences. Children then use the same age data from Day One to investigate some new questions. The questions posed today provide children with more opportunities to use a variety of strategies for subtraction, but they are also designed to prompt discussion of the relationship among different uses of subtraction: missing addend, difference, and removal. Why are some of the answers the same as on Day One, even though the questions are different?

Day Two Outline

Minilesson: Around the Circle

* Record children's answers as they add and subtract ten.
* Discuss the repeating tens pattern and encourage children to generalize.

Developing the Context

* Ask children to investigate the questions in Appendix C.

Supporting the Investigation

* Encourage the children to use strategies from today's minilesson or from their work on Day One.

Materials Needed

El Bisabuelo Gregorio (Appendix A)

Student recording sheet for the exploring ages investigation (Appendix C)—one per pair of children

Large chart pad and easel

Markers

Minilesson: Around the Circle (10–15 minutes)

☀ Record children's answers as they add and subtract ten.

☀ Discuss the repeating tens pattern and encourage children to generalize.

Gather the children in the meeting area and have them sit in a circle. Have one child choose a number between 1 and 9. Write it at the top of a large sheet of chart paper. Go around the circle having each child add 10 and record the results on the chart paper. For example, if a child chooses 3, you would be recording 13, 23, 33, 43, 53, etc. Discuss the pattern and ask, "Will this always happen?" If they are not sure, try a few more numbers such as 7 or 8, adding 10 repeatedly, as before.

Next, try subtraction. Have a child choose a number between 100 and 200. Go around the circle subtracting 10 each time. For example, if a child chooses 189, you would be recording 179, 169, 159, etc. Allow children to count backward if they need to. Don't explain the decreasing tens pattern; let them notice it. When they begin to notice it, encourage them to see the decreasing tens pattern as 17, 16, 15, etc, not just as decreasing the tens in the tens column: 7, 6, 5. This noticing will help them with the turning point of 109 to 99, where 10 becomes 9. Tease them by suggesting that the pattern only happened because the number was 189. Ask them for another number and try it again. Ask, "Will this always happen?"

Developing the Context

☀ Ask children to investigate the questions in Appendix C.

Remind the children of the investigation from Day One and ask them to work on a few more questions about Carlos's family:

- How many years until Carlos reaches the age of each person in his family?

- How many years until Maria reaches those ages?

- How old will those people be then?

- How long ago was each person 8 years old?

Have children work with the same math partners as on Day One to answer the questions about Carlos's family (Appendix C). There are many questions here and children will need much time to investigate them all. Plan on at least the whole period, if not another day, to allow them to answer all the questions.

Supporting the Investigation

☀ Encourage the children to use strategies from today's minilesson or from their work on Day One.

As you observe the children at work, focus on their strategies. Many will probably not realize that some of the answers will be the same as on Day One. Encourage them to try some of the strategies from the minilesson (plus ten, minus ten, as appropriate) or to see if the strategies discussed in the congress on Day One are helpful.

If some children easily see the connection between their work on Day One and today, remind them that they will have to prove their thinking to the community and explain how the problems are similar. The problems have been intentionally juxtaposed to help children notice patterns and ponder how the various contexts are related.

Have children save their sheets in their work folders.

Assessment Tips

As you observe and confer, note whether children's strategies are changing. More specifically, are they adding up from 8? If so, how? By tens? By ones? Do they see any relationship between the problems from Day One and today or do they solve each problem as if there were no relationships? It is helpful to jot down your observations on sticky notes. Later, you can place these on children's recording sheets to be included in their portfolios.

Differentiating Instruction

Support and challenge each pair appropriately. Children who are still counting can be challenged and supported to take leaps to landmark numbers. Children who are decomposing and using landmark numbers can be encouraged to take larger jumps (instead of 10, encourage them to try 30, or to take a very large jump and adjust at the end). To challenge those who begin to see the relationships among the problems, suggest that they work on drawing pictures on a timeline to prove their thinking—to prove how the questions are related and why the patterns on the chart are appearing.

Reflections on the Day

Today children solved several more subtraction problems. You had an opportunity to notice their strategies as you walked around and conferred. Are they using landmarks and taking leaps of ten or are they still counting? Are they able to anticipate which answers will be the same? Do they see how the problems are related? These questions get to the heart of subtraction and its relationship to addition.

DAY THREE
Exploring Ages

Materials Needed

Children's recording sheets from Days One and Two

Large chart paper—one sheet per pair of children

Sticky notes—one pad per child

Large chart pad and easel

Markers

Children are asked to look over the data they have collected thus far, focusing specifically on the patterns they notice (why many of the answers are the same, or related). Children prepare for a congress to discuss the reasons for the patterns (not to discuss their strategies as they did on Day One). They make posters and then have a "gallery walk" where they read each other's work, raise questions, and make comments.

Day Three Outline

Minilesson: Around the Circle

☀ Continue to explore the pattern that results when adding or subtracting ten.

Preparing for the Math Congress

☀ Ask children to discuss patterns in their answers from their work on Days One and Two and prepare posters to highlight their findings.

☀ Give children time to review and record comments on each other's posters.

☀ Plan a congress that will focus on constant difference and the relationship between addition and subtraction.

Minilesson: Around the Circle (10-15 minutes)

If the children were surprised by the patterns appearing in the minilesson on Day Two, repeat the same minilesson today, but have children choose different starting numbers. Continue to explore the pattern of adding and subtracting ten. Over time you want to ensure that children can do this easily and that they understand why this pattern occurs. If this understanding was evident on Day Two, then try subtracting 20 each time. What patterns appear? Why?

☀ Continue to explore the pattern that results when adding or subtracting ten.

Preparing for the Math Congress

Pass out the children's work folders. Ask them to take out the recording sheets they completed on Days One and Two and with their math partners discuss the patterns they notice in the answers. Ask them to discuss why those patterns occurred and to prepare for a math congress during which they will share their findings. Ask them to make big posters of the interesting things they have noticed and why they think those things happened.

☀ Ask children to discuss patterns in the answers from their work on Days One and Two and prepare posters to highlight their findings.

☀ Give children time to review and record comments on each other's posters.

☀ Plan a congress that will focus on constant difference and the relationship between addition and subtraction.

As the children work, walk around and take note of the things they are talking about. There are several things you can anticipate:

✦ They may notice that many of the answers are the same. When this occurs, tell children to try to come to the congress prepared to explain why this happened.

✦ Some children may try to use number lines to explore what is happening. Encourage and support them to do so. For example, the number line below shows the age of Carlos's mom when Carlos was born (25); how many years it will take for Carlos, who is 8, to become 33 (25); and how old his mom will be then, 25 years later (58). This type of representation can lead to a nice discussion of *constant difference.*

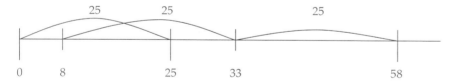

✦ Some children may talk about *the relationship between addition and subtraction.* For example, they might discuss the relationships among the following questions: how many years until Carlos is 33 [missing addend, 8 + n = 33]; how old his mom was when he was born [removal, 33 − 8 = n]; and how many years ago his mom was 8 [missing subtrahend, 33 − n = 8]. These relationships can also be represented on the number line.

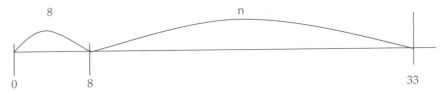

When children are ready, have them lay their posters out on tables. Allow children to walk around and look at each other's posters and place sticky notes on them with comments and/or questions for the authors/mathematicians.

■ Tips for Structuring the Math Congress

In the congress on Day Four, you will want to have a discussion on two big ideas on the landscape of learning for subtraction: constant difference and the relationship between addition and subtraction. You will also want to focus on how all the problems were related and on how subtraction can be thought of in many ways. Look over the posters and think about how you will structure discussion in the math congress. Which posters can be used to focus that discussion? Which pairs of children should share? Choose one pair for each big idea.

Reflections on the Day

Today children focused on some big ideas related to subtraction (constant difference and the relationship between addition and subtraction) and the connection between several uses for subtraction (difference, removal, missing addend, and missing subtrahend). As children reviewed each other's posters, what questions and comments did they have? The gallery walk engaged children in examining how other mathematicians communicate about their ideas. The questions and comments they receive should help them to reflect on the soundness of their arguments.

Exploring Ages

A math congress is convened to discuss the posters created on Day Three. Discussion focuses on the connections among the problems, the relationship between subtraction and addition, and constant difference.

Day Four Outline

Facilitating the Math Congress

☀ Have children discuss their posters and focus on the connections among the problems.

☀ Have children discuss their posters and focus on the connections among the problems.

The major part of the math workshop time is devoted today to a math congress.

Inside One Classroom

A Portion of the Math Congress

Matt (the teacher): Yesterday as I walked around with all of you looking at all the posters, I saw several posters showing and heard several people talking about how the problems were related. Daniel and Michelle, would you bring up your poster and start us off? What relationships did you notice?

Daniel: It's like they are opposites. One problem is 33 − 8 equals 25. And the other is 8 plus what is 33.
(As he talks he writes: 33 − 8 = 25; 8 +? = 33.)

Michelle: It's like the numbers just switch around.

Colleen: I know what they mean. I saw that, too. But why does it do that? I don't know why it is doing that and that is what is confusing me.

Matt: What is the 25 in this problem? *(Points to the first problem.)*

Daniel: That is how old the mom was when Carlos was born, and this one is how many years till he is 33.

Matt: OK, so now let's go back to Colleen's question.

Daniel: It's like if you have two numbers, and the total is 33—if you take one number away you are left with the other.

Matt: Turn to the person next to you. Talk about what Daniel just said and decide if you agree. *(Allows for a few minutes for pair talk.)*

Manuel: We agree. There's other opposites, too. 55 − 8 = 47; 55 − 47 = 8; and 8 + 47 = 55.

Emmy: But where is the 8 on the timeline? Is it the jump or is it a number on the line?

Daniel: It doesn't matter. It's still the difference between the numbers.
(He writes: 8 +? = 55 and 55 − 47 = 8.)

Michelle: And it could also be 55 − 8 = 47. That's because 47 + 8 = 55.

Continued on next page

Author's Notes

Daniel and Michelle had been discussing the relationship between addition and subtraction. By starting the congress with this pair, Matt is assured of having a rich conversation on this big idea.

Encourage children to come up and display their posters. Give them a chance to present the relationships they noticed. Help them clarify if necessary, and then allow others to comment and question.

Invite the children to discuss and prove their ideas to each other. Noticing a pattern is an important beginning, but then mathematicians work to explain why the pattern is happening and if it can be generalized.

Pair talk allows the children time to reflect on the question and it gets everyone involved.

Continued from previous page

Matt: So are we saying that subtraction and addition are related and so all of these questions are related?

Emmy: Yes. You just have to decide which part you want to know about.

Matt: Daniel, you said something about "difference." And I know some kids investigated that idea, too. Emmanuel and Maria, would you come share next…about your idea of difference?

Maria: We made lots of number lines. If you think about the difference between the numbers on them, the answers are all the same. $33 - 8 = 25$; $25 - 0 = 25$; $35 - 10 = 25$.

Ian: Oh, that's cool. It's like the problem is just sliding up and down the line! It's always the same difference, though.

Matt: Does that mean we could always just make a messy problem friendly? Like $33 - 19$. Would the answer be the same if we made it $34 - 20$? Would this strategy always work?

Push for generalization, of a discussion of the part-whole relations. Generalization gets to the heart of doing mathematics. Moments like these are to be maximized. Emmy's response shows she really understands how the parts and the whole are related—how addition is related to subtraction.

Emmanuel and Maria are asked to share next to allow for a discussion of constant difference as well.

Once again Matt pushes for generalization. Can we make messy problems friendly? How? Will this always work? Note the use of the word always.

Assessment Tips

The posters are probably too large to place in children's portfolios. If this is the case, you can take photographs of them and staple each photograph to a blank page for your anecdotal notes. You may also want to photocopy the landscape of learning graphic (page 11) and, for each child, shade in the landmarks as you find evidence in their work. Note the children you are not sure of, for whom you have no evidence. Over the next week you will want to take special note of their work.

Literacy Connection

Once the class has engaged in a rich discussion about the relationships among the problems and on clever strategies, you and the class can make your own read-aloud book—the sequel to *El Bisabuelo Gregorio.* Your book can contain all the data you found, the findings and observations of the children, the big ideas discussed about subtraction, and the strategies that the class constructed. By making this book and having it available throughout the year, you allow children to revisit and reflect on all the wonderful ideas and strategies they constructed throughout the unit.

Reflections on the Day

Children have now completed their investigations about the characters in *El Bisabuelo Gregorio.* They have used a variety of strategies to figure out several questions regarding age differences, they have collected data and analyzed it for patterns, and they have had a math congress on several important ideas and models regarding subtraction. During this time you have had opportunities to take note of their strategies, their inventions, and their struggles. This is a turning point in the unit. Now that several big ideas about subtraction have been discussed, children will be asked to consider them as they investigate their own families. Efficient computation strategies will also become the focus as the unit progresses.

Investigating Their Families

Today's minilesson encourages children to think about when adding on might be helpful, versus when removing is more helpful. When numbers are close together, it is often helpful to add on; for example, when solving $42 - 35$, it is easy to add on from the 35. In contrast, adding on would not be a very helpful strategy for $42 - 6$. In this case it is easier to remove 6. After the minilesson, children cut out ten-strips and build a timeline. They then figure out the years in which they were born and add that to their timelines.

Day Five Outline

Minilesson: A Subtraction String

☀ Work on a string of related problems designed to highlight the efficient use of adding on and removing.

☀ Record children's strategies on an open number line.

Developing the Context

☀ Ask children to find out in what years their family members were born.

☀ Make a timeline with landmark numbers on it.

Supporting the Investigation

☀ Help children make their own timelines, including the current year and the year in which they were born.

Materials Needed

Strips of ten (Appendix D)— one set per child

Before class you should also make two copies of Appendix D and cut out and tape several of the strips together for whole-class use.

Large chart pad and easel

Markers

Scissors— one pair per child

Tape—for each child

Minilesson: A Subtraction String (10–15 minutes)

- Work on a string of related problems designed to highlight the efficient use of adding on and removing.

- Record children's strategies on an open number line.

This mental math minilesson uses a string of related problems to encourage children to explore how it is easier to remove when numbers are far apart and add on when numbers are close together. Do one problem at a time and record children's strategies on the open number line, inviting other children to comment on the representations. As you progress through the string and you notice children varying their strategies, invite a discussion on why they might be removing sometimes and adding on at other times. If the class comes to a consensus that it is easier to add on when numbers are close together and remove when they are far apart, you might want to make a sign about this and post it in the meeting area. Over time you can have several signs labeled "Helpful Subtraction Strategies" posted on the wall.

Behind the Numbers

The problems and numbers in the string were chosen carefully. They vary in whether the numbers are far apart or close together. The string is structured to encourage children to examine the numbers first before they decide on a strategy—to explicitly focus on when it is helpful to remove and when it is helpful to add on. Do not start the string with this discussion, however. Let the discussion emerge naturally after the third or fourth problem.

String of related problems:

$$82 - 6$$

$$64 - 59$$

$$56 - 8$$

$$94 - 89$$

$$132 - 128$$

$$135 - 13$$

Inside One Classroom

A Portion of the Minilesson

Matt (the teacher): Here's our first warm-up problem: $82 - 6 = ?$. Thumbs-up when you have an answer. *(After think time.)* Michael?

Michael: It's 76. I counted back. 81, 80, 79, 78, 77, 76.

(Matt draws the following representation of Michael's strategy:)

Author's Notes

Think time allows children time to solve the problem, and the thumbs-up signal gives Matt a way to judge how much time is needed.

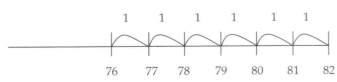

Continued on next page

Continued on next page

Matt: Does everyone agree with Michael? *(No disagreement is apparent.)* Does anyone have a way to do that one with fewer steps? Your way works, Michael, but it was a lot of counting that you needed to keep track of. Emmy?

Emmy: I did a jump of 2, and then 4.

Matt: Let's see what that looks like on the number line. *(Using Michael's number line, records the jumps in a different color:)*

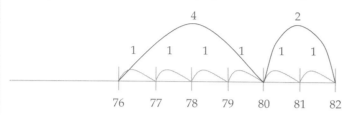

Matt: What do you think, Michael? Does Emmy's way work? Saves a lot of counting, doesn't it? OK, let's go on to the next problem: $64 - 59 = ?$. Show me with your thumb when you are ready. Susie?

Susie: It's 5. I just thought of the difference. It's 1 to get to 60, then 4 more.

Matt: Nice. You used a landmark number to help, too, like Emmy. Let me record your strategy.

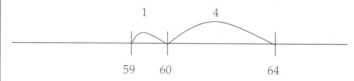

Matt: Here's the next one: $56 - 8 =$. Michael, want to try taking leaps? What's a nice landmark number here?

Michael: Fifty. I could do a jump of 6 to get there, then…

Matt: How many more do you need to take away? We want to take 8 away.

Michael: Two, I think.

Matt: I'll make a picture. Let's be sure.

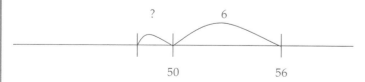

Asking if anyone has a way to do it with fewer steps suggests that efficiency might be important to consider. Pedagogical moves like this also imply that while answers are important, how they are derived is an important focus of examination.

By using the same number line, but a different color, a representation is created that allows children to reflect on how the strategies shared thus far are related.

Matt returns to Michael to encourage him to abandon his counting strategy and to attempt decomposing using landmarks.

Continued on next page

Continued from previous page

Michael: It is 2, 'cause 6 + 2 is 8.

(Matt draws the following to complete the problem:)

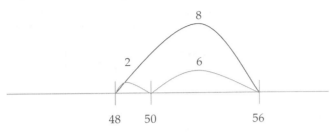

Matt: So 48. I have another question. It seems like sometimes we are going forward, adding, and other times we are going backward. Talk to the person next to you about this. Why switch your strategy? *(Allows a few minutes of pair talk.)*

At this point the main purpose of the string is put forth for discussion.

Manuel: When the numbers are close together, it is easier to add up. When they are far apart, like 56 and 8, it is easier to go back.

Matt: How many of you agree with Manuel? Let's think about this as we continue with our string. If we agree at the end, we can make a sign and post it on our "Helpful Subtraction Strategies" wall.

Developing the Context

☀ Ask children to find out in what years their family members were born.

☀ Make a timeline with landmark numbers on it.

Tell the children that now that they have developed so many strategies and ideas about subtraction, they will each be investigating the ages of their own family members. Tonight when they go home, they should interview people in their families to find out the years in which they were born.

Note: Family structures today can be very diverse. It is important to be sensitive to this fact. Some of the children in your class may not live with their parents, many may not have siblings, and others may live with aunts or uncles, foster parents, or may even be in shelters. It is important to construe the notion of "family" liberally and encourage children to collect data on the people around them, relatives, friends, babysitters, etc.

Take the strips of ten you prepared before math workshop and tape it across the chalkboard. Explain to the children that you have made a timeline and now you are going to put some landmark numbers on it. On the chalkboard, mark each decade where the strips attach. Write the current year on the bottom half of one of the small rectangular tabs. Ask the children to help you find where to place it on the timeline. Write landmark years on the other tabs and tape the tabs onto the timeline as shown below.

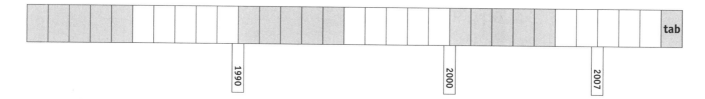

Supporting the Investigation

Pass out a set of ten-strips and tabs (Appendix D) to each child. Ask the children to cut out the pieces and make a timeline like yours. Have them place the current year on it as you did, and then ask them to figure out the year in which they were born and place that on it as well. When they are finished, have them place their timelines in their work folders.

Move around the room, helping children as needed. Note the strategies they are using to figure out when they were born: are they counting backward by ones, making use of the five-structure, or making jumps to landmark decades?

Bring the class back together for a short discussion on the different strategies. Use the open number line to represent the various strategies.

☀ Help children make their own timelines, including the current year and the year they were born.

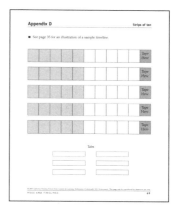

Reflections on the Day

Today children were encouraged in a minilesson to look to the numbers first before they decide on a subtraction strategy. Think about the strategies you saw them using. Are they using landmark numbers, varying their strategies? Were they able to work with large numbers when they calculated the year in which they were born?

Investigating Their Families

Materials Needed

Student recording sheet for the family ages investigation (Appendix E)— one per child

Student work folders with timelines from Day Five

Large chart pad and easel

Markers

The day begins with a minilesson designed to encourage children to take leaps of ten or use landmark numbers—for example, to solve 34 – 19 by subtracting 20 and then adding 1. Strategies are shared, recorded on the open number line, and discussed. Children then set to work to figure out the ages of all their family members, given the birth year data they have collected.

Day Six Outline

Minilesson: A Subtraction String

☀ Work on a string of related problems designed to encourage the use of leaps of ten or landmark numbers.

☀ Record children's strategies on an open number line.

Supporting the Investigation (continued from Day Five)

☀ Have children add their family members' birth years to their timelines.

☀ Note children's strategies as they work on Appendix E.

Minilesson: A Subtraction String (10–15 minutes)

This mental math minilesson uses a string of related problems to encourage the subtraction strategy of using leaps of ten and/or landmark numbers. Do one problem at a time and record children's strategies on an open number line, inviting other children to comment on the representations and to share alternative strategies. Explore the different strategies the children offer, while at the same time encouraging them to examine the relationships among the problems. If you notice children beginning to make use of the related problems as you progress through the string, invite a discussion on how helpful it might be to do that and to take leaps of ten and/or to use landmark numbers. If the class agrees that these are helpful strategies, you might want to make a sign about this and add it to your wall of "Helpful Subtraction Strategies."

☀ Work on a string of related problems designed to encourage the use of leaps of ten or landmark numbers.

☀ Record children's strategies on an open number line.

String of related problems:

156 – 10
156 – 12
147 – 20
147 – 19
122 – 40
122 – 39
181 – 49

Behind the Numbers

The problems are structured in pairs to encourage children to use one as a support for the other. The last problem has no helper problem in the string. Children now need to think about whether the strategy they have been discussing can be used to make the problem friendlier.

Supporting the Investigation
(continued from Day Five)

Pass out children's work folders with the timelines created on Day Five and have children return to work areas. Using the data from the interviews they did at home, children should place their family members' names on their timelines at the years in which they were born, similar to how they placed themselves on Day Five.

Pass out a student recording sheet (Appendix E) to each child. The children will complete it by figuring out the age of each family member.

☀ Have children add their family members' birth years to their timelines.

☀ Note children's strategies as they work on Appendix E.

■ Assessment Tips

Note the strategies children are using to figure out how old each family member is. Remember to pay particular attention to the children for whom you feel you do not have enough evidence. As the unit progresses, also pay particular attention to the growth and development children are making and note it on the landscape of learning graphic.

Differentiating Instruction

For children who are struggling to count, help them use the timeline as a manipulative and encourage them either to count on with it or to make leaps to landmark numbers, using the five- or ten-structure. Encourage those who are already taking leaps to landmark numbers to take even bigger leaps. For example, when figuring the difference between 1972 and 2006, instead of adding 10 repeatedly, encourage them to add a chunk of 30 at once. Encourage children who are already taking chunks to use constant difference and turn the problem into 2004 – 1970.

Reflections on the Day

The minilesson today encouraged children to use landmarks and to remove groups of ten. When children calculated the ages of the people in their families, what strategies for subtraction did you notice? Are they varying their strategies depending on the numbers? Do they make use of landmarks? Do they add on when appropriate and remove when appropriate? Are they developing a repertoire of strategies for subtraction?

Investigating Their Families

Today's mental math minilesson is designed to encourage the use of constant difference—making equivalent but friendlier problems by sliding up and down the number line. After the minilesson, children will work to figure out how old each family member was when the child was born and how old each family member will be when the child becomes 10 and then 20. These contexts support the development and consolidation of children's understanding of subtraction as difference.

Materials Needed

Student recording sheets for the family ages investigation (Appendix F)—one set per child

Large chart pad and easel

Markers

Day Seven Outline

Minilesson: A Subtraction String

* Work on a string of related problems designed to highlight constant difference.
* Record children's strategies on an open number line.

Developing the Context

* Inform the children that they will be making a book about the ages of their family members.
* Preview the problems in Appendix F.

Supporting the Investigation

* Encourage the children to consider flexible and efficient strategies.

Minilesson: A Subtraction String (10–15 minutes)

☀ Work on a string of related problems designed to highlight constant difference.

☀ Record children's strategies on an open number line.

This mental math minilesson uses a string of related problems to encourage children to explore constant difference as a way to make problems friendlier. Do one problem at a time and record children's strategies on the open number line, inviting other children to comment on the representations and to share alternative strategies. If you notice children beginning to make use of the related problems as you progress through the string, invite a discussion on how helpful it might be to do that, and how thinking about subtraction as age differences and as sliding up and down the number line might make it easier. Suggest that they try to make problems into friendlier ones, like mathematicians! If the class agrees that these are helpful strategies, you might want to add them to your wall of "Helpful Subtraction Strategies."

Behind the Numbers

The first four problems in this string are all related in ways that will support and encourage children to think about constant difference. After the fourth problem, if they have not yet noticed the relationships, include some more problems, such as $68 - 33$, $73 - 38$, and $74 - 39$. Once it becomes apparent that the answers are all the same, discuss why that is happening. Represent the problems on the number line as constant difference (not as removal) and discuss how you are just sliding up and down the number line to solve the problems—that the difference is staying the same. You can also put the numbers in the context of age differences, for example, by saying, "My mom is 70 and I am 35. When I am 36, she will be 71." Once children understand the strategy, encourage them to use it to make the last two problems friendlier. For example, $152 - 49$ becomes an easy problem to solve when you realize it is equivalent to $153 - 50$.

String of related problems:

$$70 - 35$$
$$71 - 36$$
$$72 - 37$$
$$69 - 34$$
$$152 - 49$$
$$174 - 59$$

Developing the Context

☀ Inform the children that they will be making a book about the ages of their family members.

☀ Preview the problems in Appendix F.

Tell the children that over the next several days they will be involved in making a book about the ages of their family members—a book like Carlos made for Bisabuelo Gregorio. The first page will be the sheet they completed on Day Six (Appendix E). Today they will figure out how old their family members were when the children were born and how old their family members will be when the children are 10 and 20. Use the recording sheets in Appendix F. It is helpful if you do a book on your family as well. At the end of this unit when the children share their books, they will enjoy hearing yours, too. (Some teachers prefer to make their book right away and read it on Day Six or Seven, to develop the context for the bookmaking.)

Supporting the Investigation

Move around the room, conferring with and supporting children as needed. Remember that your goal is to work with the mathematicians, not just to fix their answers. Help them develop flexibility, number sense, and efficient strategies. Help them think about how the age difference is staying the same.

☀ Encourage the children to consider flexible and efficient strategies.

▨ Assessment Tips

Note the strategies that the children are using: are they still counting backward or forward by ones or are they making use of the five-structure, making large jumps, using landmark decades, or using constant difference? Remember to pay particular attention to the children for whom you do not yet have enough evidence. As the unit progresses, pay particular attention to the growth and development children are making and note it on the landscape of learning graphic.

Differentiating Instruction

As you confer, differentiate by supporting and helping children in developmentally appropriate ways. For children who are struggling to count, help them use the timeline as a manipulative and encourage them either to count on with it or to make leaps to landmark numbers, using the five- or ten-structure. With those who are already taking leaps to landmark numbers, encourage them to take bigger leaps. For children who can already take chunks at once, encourage them to use constant difference.

Reflections on the Day

The focus of the work today was on constant difference as a strategy and on the relationship between removal (mom's age when child was born) and difference (difference between mom's and child's ages) problems. Many children may have removed 8 from the age of their family members to determine how old they were at the children's birth. The children may have been surprised to discover that the result was the difference in ages, the amount that needed to be added to 10 and then to 20 to answer the other questions. Puzzling over the relationships in these problems brings children to a deeper understanding of subtraction.

DAY EIGHT

Investigating Their Families

Materials Needed

Student recording sheet for the family ages investigation (Appendix G)—one per child

Children's recording sheets from Day Seven

Large chart pad and easel

Markers

The minilesson today continues to support the development of constant difference. Today's investigation invites children to consider how old their family members will be when the children reach the age their family members are now. The children also investigate how many years it will take for them to become the current age of each family member. Once again the connection between various subtraction problems is the focus, and missing addend is now connected to difference.

Day Eight Outline

Minilesson: A Subtraction String

☀ Work on a string of related problems designed to reinforce constant difference.

☀ Record children's strategies on an open number line.

Developing the Context

☀ Have a few children share their findings from Day Seven, focusing particularly on constant difference.

☀ Preview the problems in Appendix G.

Supporting the Investigation

☀ Help children make connections to their previous work and encourage them to explain their findings.

Minilesson: A Subtraction String (10–15 minutes)

This mental math minilesson uses a string of related problems to encourage children to continue to explore constant difference. As before, do one problem at a time and record children's strategies on the open number line, inviting other children to comment on the representations and to share alternative strategies.

String of related problems:

90 – 40

91 – 39

91 – 41

52 – 38

54 – 40

63 – 38

172 – 49

174 – 89

- ☀ Work on a string of related problems designed to reinforce constant difference.
- ☀ Record children's strategies on an open number line.

Behind the Numbers

The first three problems in this string are designed to support a discussion of constant difference right from the start. The first one is easy, while the second may cause children to make errors (91 is an increase of 1, while 39 is a decrease of 1; thus the answer is 52, not 50). It has been placed here intentionally to give you a chance to process the errors on the number line and to explore constant difference once again. The third problem, when contrasted with the second, will refocus the conversation on what is happening. Represent the problems on the number line as constant difference (not as removal) and discuss how the problems involve sliding up and down the number line—that the difference is staying the same. Remember that you can also put the numbers in the context of age differences. Encourage children to use strategies to make the problems friendlier.

Developing the Context

Start by having a few children read from their work of Day Seven and share some of their observations, particularly about constant difference. Record some of the children's work on an open number line and discuss how the differences stayed the same. Have the other children review their own work to see if that happened with their data as well.

Tell them that today they will work to figure out how many years it will be until they reach the age of the other people in their book, and how old those people will be then (see Appendix G). When completed, this page will be added to their books.

- ☀ Have a few children share their findings from Day Seven, focusing particularly on constant difference.
- ☀ Preview the problems in Appendix G.

Supporting the Investigation

Confer with children and support them as needed. Remember that your goal is to work with the mathematicians, not just to fix their answers. Help them develop flexibility, number sense, and efficient strategies. Encourage them to wonder why the results are similar and to explain what is happening. Help them connect missing addend problems (how many years until) to difference (difference in ages) and removal problems (age of mom when child was born.)

- ☀ Help children make connections to their previous work and encourage them to explain their findings.

■ Assessment Tips

As you move around the room, note the strategies children are using: are they still counting backward or forward by ones or are they using the five-structure, large jumps, landmark numbers, and constant difference? Do they know immediately that the answer to the first question—how many years it will be until they are the age of each family member—can be answered with the results of their work from Day Seven? Remember to pay particular attention to the children for whom you do not yet have enough evidence. As the unit progresses, also pay particular attention to the growth and development children are making and note it on the landscape of learning graphic.

Differentiating Instruction

As you confer, differentiate by supporting and helping children in developmentally appropriate ways. For children who are struggling to count, help them use the timeline as a manipulative and encourage them to either count on with it or to make leaps to landmark numbers, using the five- or ten-structure. With those who are already taking leaps to landmark numbers, encourage them to take bigger leaps. For children who can already take chunks at once, encourage them to use constant difference.

At this point, some children may already see all the relationships, and they may see no need to calculate the answers to the new problems, as the answers are apparent from the start. As an extension, ask these children to write up biographies of some famous people. The biographies should include the year they were born, the year they died, how old they were when they died, etc.

You can also have children use the ten-strips to record the age of an elder, such as someone else in the community, a neighbor, or a friend of the family. Have them compare age data for all their elders. You might also add yours or those of other community elders. Place the strips above the timeline showing when they were born. Consider using different length strips and discussing equivalence. For example, strips of 25 could be used as well: 87 could be represented as 8 tens and 7 units or as 4 twenty-fives minus 13.

Reflections on the Day

Children have now explored various subtraction problems and developed several strategies for computation. Today they had a chance to work on constant difference, to explore missing addend problems, and to discover that the age difference is always the same. Now is a good point for you to take note of the children who have a strong understanding and those who are still struggling. Where is each child on the landscape? On Day Nine you will have a chance to do some further assessment.

Assessment

Today is a day for assessment. The minilesson allows you to assess informally while teaching: to see how the children vary their strategies for subtraction. Because the problems in the minilesson string are not related, children will need to look to the numbers and choose an appropriate strategy. As they work on the last pages of their books, they will also be varying their strategies and writing about them. These last pages allow you to capture the mathematizing formally and to see what subtraction strategies each child has developed.

Day Nine Outline

Minilesson: A Subtraction String

* Work through a string of unrelated problems designed to help you assess the development of children's strategies.

Developing the Context

* Preview the problems in Appendix H, explaining that these will be the final pages in their family ages books.

Supporting the Investigation

* Celebrate the development of the children's strategies.
* Help children compile their family ages books.

Materials Needed

Student recording sheets for subtraction strategies (Appendix H)—one set per child

Drawing paper—one sheet per child

Children's recording sheets from Days Six, Seven, and Eight

Large chart pad and easel

Markers

Minilesson: A Subtraction String (10–15 minutes)

☀ Work through a string of unrelated problems designed to help you assess the development of children's strategies.

This mental math minilesson includes many problems that can be made easier with constant difference. However, the string is not organized in a specific fashion to support one strategy over another. As with previous strings, do one problem at a time and record children's strategies on the open number line, inviting other children to comment on the representations and to share alternative strategies.

String of problems:

2006 – 1999

1999 – 1987

1992 – 8

52 – 6

54 – 29

63 – 38

172 – 45

174 – 89

Behind the Numbers

The numbers have been chosen carefully so that you can see whether children choose a strategy that is helpful given the numbers. Do they use the same strategy for every problem? Or, do they look to the numbers first and choose a strategy that makes sense, given the numbers? For example, a nice strategy for 1992 – 8 is to go back 2 and then 6. However, this would not be a good strategy for 2006 – 1999. Here it makes more sense to add on to 1999, or to use constant difference: 2007 – 2000. Since the problems are not specifically related, this will be a good chance to notice and assess the subtraction strategies children have in their toolboxes.

☀ Preview the problems in Appendix H, explaining that these will be the final pages in their family ages books.

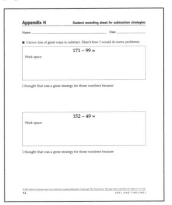

Developing the Context

Tell the children that today they will work on the last pages for their books. On these pages, children will solve several subtraction problems and explain the strategies they have learned as they progressed through this unit. Pass out the recording sheets (Appendix H) as well as sheets of drawing paper that they can use as covers for their books.

Supporting the Investigation

Help children put their pages in order. When the unit is over you can have them draw a picture of their families for the cover. Note the strategies they are writing about and celebrate their accomplishments with them.

Assessment Tips

This activity is designed as an individual assessment. Workspace is provided for each of the problems so you can see the strategies each child uses. Make copies of these pages and place them in the child's portfolio. Note the strategies, paying particular attention to children's growth and development. Color in the landmarks on the landscape of learning graphic to record where each child is on the journey.

Reflections on the Day

Today you collected evidence of the wonderful subtraction strategies your children have developed. Examine the landscape of learning graphic and note where each child is. Does each child have a toolbox of strategies? Does the child look to the numbers first before choosing a strategy? Are the chosen strategies representative of good number sense?

☀ Celebrate the development of the children's strategies.

☀ Help children compile their family ages books.

Celebrating the Mathematicians' Stories

Materials Needed

Completed children's books

Today is a day for celebration and a chance for your young mathematicians to share what they have been doing and learning. You and the children will be hosting a celebration similar to the one described in the book *El Bisabuelo Gregorio.*

The Celebration

Invite parents, the principal, and interested others to hear the stories the children have written. Just as in the story *El Bisabuelo Gregorio,* children can present their families with their books as gifts. The children can now serve as experts to help other children in the school do a similar project.

As the children progressed through this unit, they constructed many big ideas about subtraction and a variety of strategies for mental arithmetic. Most parents will likely only use standard algorithms; they may in fact see these algorithms as the goal of instruction. This is your chance to help parents understand the importance of mental arithmetic in today's world and see and appreciate the variety of strategies their children have been learning.

Reflections on the Unit

The mathematician Samuel Karlin once wrote, "The purpose of models is not to fit the data but to sharpen the questions" (1983). This unit introduced the open number line as a powerful model for sharpening questions about number relations and operations. Children explored the topic of subtraction, developed several strategies, and used the number line model to represent the relationship between addition and subtraction and to explore how the operation of subtraction can be employed in solving various problems—such as removal, comparative difference, and finding a missing addend.

This model can now be used throughout the year as you continue to work on addition and subtraction. Another unit in the *Contexts for Learning Mathematics* series, *Minilessons for Extending Addition and Subtraction,* can be a helpful resource as you continue to plan strings of related problems for minilessons and use the open number line to record children's strategies.

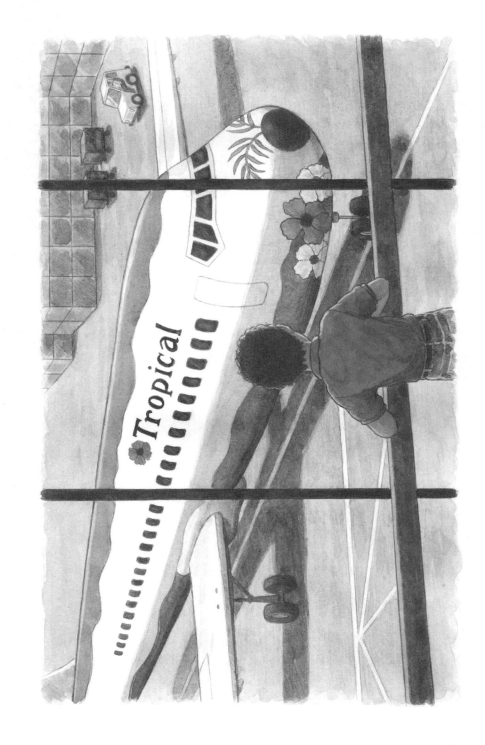

It all happened the day Carlos turned eight! His great-grandfather, Bisabuelo Gregorio, came on an airplane all the way from Puerto Rico to New York, where Carlos lived, just for his birthday.

Carlos had never seen a man with such thick, wavy, beautiful silver hair before; he knew el bisabuelo must be very old. Carlos hoped he would have beautiful silver hair like that some day and he wondered how many birthdays would need to pass for that to happen.

"Ocho añitos . . . eight years old. I was your age once, you know," el bisabuelo said with a twinkle in his eye. "That was seventy-nine years ago!"

"Did you have a party like me?" Carlos asked shyly. El bisabuelo leaned back in his chair, closed his eyes, and began to rock gently. At first Carlos thought maybe he was falling asleep. But Bisabuelo Gregorio was remembering his eighth birthday, and it seemed like just yesterday. He could see his cake and his whole family sitting around a table in the kitchen—the kitchen in the old house in Esperanza—the one he knew so well as a young boy. He saw the swooping palms and remembered the wild horses that roamed the island. On his eighth birthday he and his friend Luis had caught one. They named the horse Amigo and tamed him, and they rode him all around the island. But that was a long time ago. Gregorio lived in the big city of San Juan now. Still, he could almost feel the balmy breeze across his cheek and taste the sweet ripe mangoes when he thought of Esperanza. His eyes began to glisten and he reached over and put his arm around Carlos. "Sí, sí, muchacho. Just like you. Seventy-nine years ago," he said. "But like yesterday."

Carlos began to wonder, "If he was eight years old seventy-nine years ago, can I figure out how old he is now?" He thought, "79 + 8. That's 79 and 1, that's 80, and then 7 more. 87!" Was he right?

And that was when it happened. The whole family started talking at once about when they were eight. They told about where they lived, who their friends were, and what they did. First, el Bisabuelo Gregorio told about when he was eight, about his friend Luis and the horse, Amigo. And then Grandma Rosita told about how she had the chicken pox on her eighth birthday and how she was too sick to eat her cake. Carlos began wondering how many years ago it was that mamá y papá, his mom and dad, turned eight. Did they have a birthday party, too? Did Grandma Rosita make a big birthday cake for his mamá? It was hard for him to even imagine his mamá as a little girl of eight. What did she look like?

The questions kept coming and wouldn't stop. He began to wonder how old his mamá was when he was born. How old was Grandpa Juan? How many years until Carlos would be as old as el bisabuelo . . . when he might have silver hair like that? How many years until his mamá y papá would be eighty-seven? Would his dad have silver hair like el Bisabuelo Gregorio?

And then Carlos had an idea. He would make a big chart with everyone's age on it and use the chart to help him answer all the questions. He would write a book about his family and put a big timeline in it. And then he would give the book to Bisabuelo Gregorio as a present.

He told his sister Maria and his mamá about his idea and they said they would help.

"I'm ten," Maria said. "Write that down."

His mamá said, "I'm thirty-three and your papá is thirty-five, and Grandpa Juan is fifty-five, and Grandma Rosita is fifty-seven."

Carlos wrote down all the numbers on his chart: 8 for himself, 10 for Maria, 33 for his mamá, 35 for his papá, 55 for Grandpa Juan, 57 for Grandma Rosita, and 87 for Bisabuelo Gregorio, because seventy-nine years ago he was eight so he must be eighty-seven now. "There, all organized," he thought. "Now I can start to work on the questions."

At school the next day, Carlos told his teacher about his birthday, about el Bisabuelo Gregorio, his wavy silver hair, and all the questions. Carlos's teacher, Mr. Melendez, put up Carlos's chart on the classroom wall and pretty soon the whole class was working on the questions.

"I have an idea," Mr. Melendez said. "Let's all work on our own families and make books about them. Let's explore ages! Interview your family members and find out how old they are." Carlos had started a big class project!

The next day all the kids came in with the data from their interviews and everyone started making charts—charts for their books, and charts all over the room. Everyone was excited. Suzannah had found out that her mom was twenty-eight when she was born and that was exactly the same age as Peter's mom when he was born! She put that into the book she was writing, made a chart, and drew a picture for it.

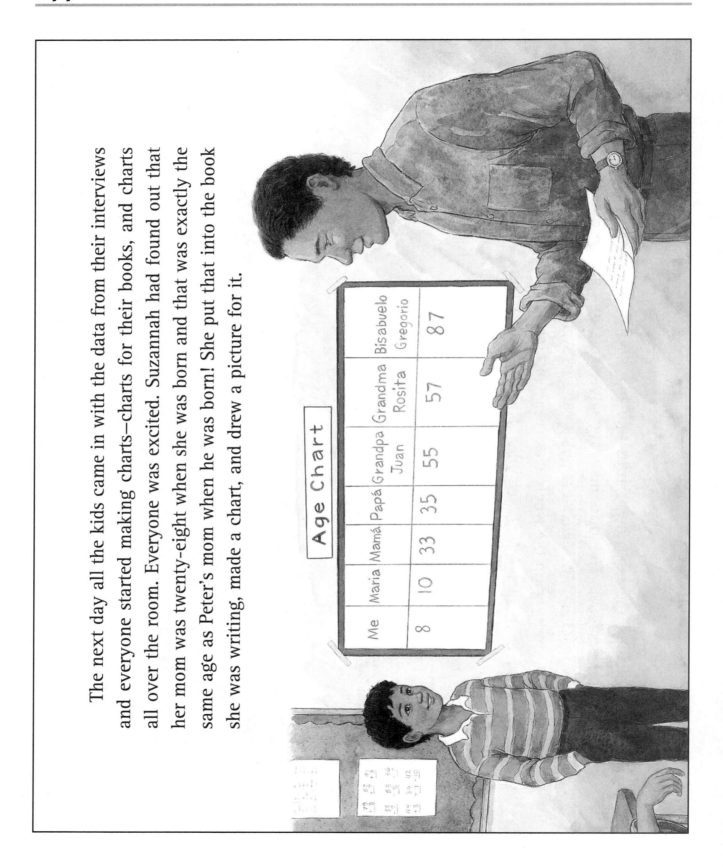

Age Chart					
Me	Maria	Mamá	Papá	Grandpa Juan	Grandma Rosita	Bisabuelo Gregorio
8	10	33	35	55	57	87

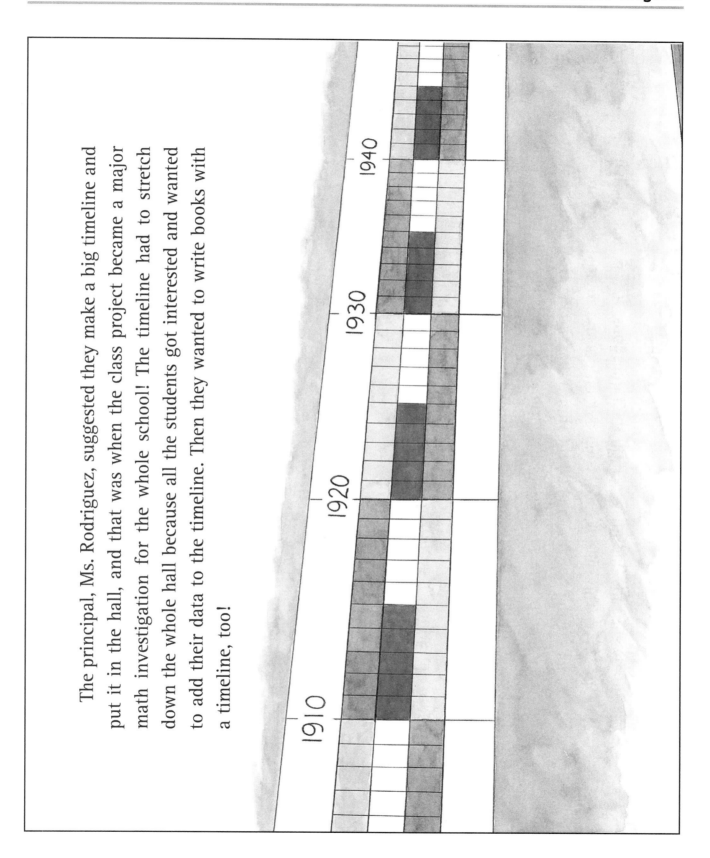

The principal, Ms. Rodriguez, suggested they make a big timeline and put it in the hall, and that was when the class project became a major math investigation for the whole school! The timeline had to stretch down the whole hall because all the students got interested and wanted to add their data to the timeline. Then they wanted to write books with a timeline, too!

Finally the kids had answered all their questions. It was time to share their answers. The school held a big exhibition and invited everyone to come and see the timeline and all the things that the kids had figured out.

At the end of the evening, Ms. Rodriguez asked everyone to join her in the auditorium. When everyone had found a seat, she said, "This has been a very special night. As you can see, all the children have worked very hard, making charts and timelines, exploring ages, and answering many questions. And now they each have a gift to give to you."

And that was the special moment. All the kids gave their books to their families and everyone began hugging and kissing.

Carlos gave his book to Bisabuelo Gregorio. Inside, on one of the pages, Carlos had written, "Mi Bisabuelo Gregorio is 87. When I was born, he was 79 years old. And 79 years ago, he was 8, and he had a birthday party." And there on the page, Carlos had drawn a beautiful picture of Amigo, the swooping palms, and Esperanza.

Mi Bisabuelo Gregorio is 87. When I was born, he was 79 years ago. And he had a birthday party. When I was old. And he was 8, and he 79 years ago.

Bisabuelo Gregorio's eyes began to water. Gently he ran his wrinkled hand over the page. "Oh, muchacho, muchacho, muchacho, gracias, gracias. Thank you, little one. You have given me precious memories—the best present ever."

Appendix B

Names _____ Date _____

Carlos	Maria	Mom	Dad	Grandpa Juan	Grandma Rosita	Bisabuelo Gregorio
8	10	33	35	55	57	87

■ How old was everyone when Carlos was born?

His sister Maria was _____.

His mom was _____.

His dad was _____.

His Grandpa Juan was _____.

His Grandma Rosita was _____.

Bisabuelo Gregorio was _____.

Names _____ Date _____

Carlos	Maria	Mom	Dad	Grandpa Juan	Grandma Rosita	Bisabuelo Gregorio
8	10	33	35	55	57	87

■ How old was everyone when Maria was born?

Her mom was _____.

Her dad was _____.

Her Grandpa Juan was _____.

Her Grandma Rosita was _____.

Bisabuelo Gregorio was _____.

Names _____ Date _____

Carlos	Maria	Mom	Dad	Grandpa Juan	Grandma Rosita	Bisabuelo Gregorio
8	10	33	35	55	57	87

■ How many years until Carlos reaches the age of each person in his family?

Maria _____   Mom _____   Dad _____   Grandpa Juan _____

Grandma Rosita _____   Bisabuelo Gregorio _____

■ How many years until Maria reaches those ages?

Mom _____   Dad _____   Grandpa Juan _____

Grandma Rosita _____   Bisabuelo Gregorio _____

■ How old will those people be then?

Mom _____   Dad _____   Grandpa Juan _____

Grandma Rosita _____   Bisabuelo Gregorio _____

■ How long ago was each person 8 years old?

Maria _____   Mom _____   Dad _____   Grandpa Juan _____

Grandma Rosita _____   Bisabuelo Gregorio _____

■ See page 35 for an illustration of a sample timeline.

									Tape Here
									Tape Here
									Tape Here
									Tape Here
									Tape Here

Tabs

Name _____ Date _____

■ These are all the people in my family and how old they are now.

Appendix F

Student recording sheet for the family ages investigation (Day Seven)

Name ______________________________ Date ______________

■ I am ______ years old. This is how old everyone was when I was born.

Name ______________________________ Age ______________

Name ______________________________ Age ______________

Name ______________________________ Age ______________

Name ______________________________ Age ______________

Name _____ Date _____

■ These are all the people in my family and how old they are now.

■ In 10 years, this is how old I will be.

■ This is how old they will be then.

■ In 20 years, this is how old I will be.

■ This is how old they will be then.

Name _____ Date _____

- ■ These are all the people in my family and how old they are now.

- ■ This is how many years it will take for me to become that old.

- ■ This is how old they will be then.

Student recording sheet for subtraction strategies

Name _____ Date _____

■ I know lots of great ways to subtract. Here's how I would do some problems:

$$171 - 99 =$$

Work space

I thought that was a great strategy for these numbers because

_____

_____

_____

$$152 - 49 =$$

Work space

I thought that was a great strategy for these numbers because

_____

_____

_____

Name _____   Date _____

$$2006 - 8 =$$

Work space

I thought that was a great strategy for these numbers because

_____

_____

_____

$$2006 - 1992 =$$

Work space

I thought that was a great strategy for these numbers because

_____

_____

_____

_____